Science Dictionary
of
DINOSAURS

Second Edition

by James Richardson
illustrated by Kaye Quinn

This second revised edition published in 2001.

Copyright © 1992 by RGA Publishing Group, Inc.

Published by Troll Communications L.L.C.

All rights reserved. No part of this book may be reproduced or utilized in any form or by any means, electronic or mechanical, including photocopying, recording, or by any information storage and retrieval system, without written permission from the publisher.

Printed in the United States of America.

10 9 8 7 6 5 4

Allosaurus (al-o-SORE-us)

Fierce meat-eating Allosaurus ("other lizard") was nearly thirty-nine feet long and weighed about four tons. This creature had a bony ridge from between its eyes to its snout, and its large jaws were lined with many sharp teeth. Allosaurus lived in what is now North America. **Late Jurassic**

Ammosaurus (am-o-SORE-us)

This seven-foot-long dinosaur had blunt teeth. It was mainly a plant-eater but may have sometimes eaten meat. Ammosaurus ("sand lizard") was named for the sandstone of northern Arizona where its fossil remains were discovered. **Late Triassic/Early Jurassic**

anatomy (uh-NAT-o-mee)

Anatomy is the study of how the parts of an animal's body go together. Knowing basic anatomy helps scientists figure out from fossil remains what a dinosaur looked like.

Anatosaurus   (uh-NAT-o-SORE-us)

Anatosaurus ("duck lizard") belonged to a dinosaur family called the duck-bills. Its mouth was shaped something like a duck's bill and lined with teeth for grinding plants. Anatosaurus was about thirty feet long, weighed three tons, and was closely related to Edmontosaurus. **Late Cretaceous**

Anchiceratops   (AN-kee-SAIR-uh-tops)

This dinosaur was a member of the Ceratops family. All Ceratopsians had horns. The Anchiceratops ("near-horned face") had very long horns above its eyes. It had a frill that protected its neck and back, and a parrotlike beak to tear up the plants it ate. **Cretaceous**

ankylosaurs   (an-KY-lo-sorz)

Ankylosaurs ("fused lizards") were armored dinosaurs that had bony plates or knobs in their skin for protection from predators. Some had spines on their sides and back. Some had tails that ended in bony clubs. The largest were more than thirty feet long. **Cretaceous**

Apatosaurus   (uh-PAT-o-SORE-us)

Apatosaurus ("deceptive lizard") was seventy feet long and weighed thirty tons. This dinosaur ate the leaves of plants that it swallowed without chewing. The leaves were ground up by small rocks, called gastroliths, in the animal's stomach. Apatosaurus is also known as Brontosaurus. **Late Jurassic**

Archaeopteryx   (ar-kee-OP-ter-iks)

Archaeopteryx ("ancient wing") combined dinosaur features and bird features in one animal. Although it had feathers like a bird, its jaws were lined with sharp teeth like those of a reptile. Archaeopteryx probably could not fly well and may have used its wings to trap the insects it ate. **Late Jurassic**

Archelon   (AR-kee-lon)

This sea turtle lived at the same time as the dinosaurs. Its shell helped to protect it from predators, and its powerful front flippers helped propel it through the water. The twelve-foot-long Archelon ("ruler turtle") ate a diet of fish. **Late Cretaceous**

archosaurs   (AR-ko-sorz)

Archosaurs ("ruling lizards") are a very large subclass of prehistoric reptiles. Archosaurs lived during the Mesozoic era and included dinosaurs, pterosaurs, crocodilians, and others.

Avimimus   (ah-vee-MY-mus)

Avimimus ("bird mimic") was a small dinosaur that looked like a modern bird with sharp teeth. This five-foot-long creature had long, powerful back legs for chasing insects and other small animals that it ate. Some scientists think it may have even had feathers, but it is not likely that Avimimus could fly. **Late Cretaceous**

Bactrosaurus (BACK-tro-SORE-us)

Although the Bactrosaurus ("club-spined lizard") was related to the duck-billed dinosaur family, its snout was very narrow. However, like other duck-bills, this dinosaur had flat teeth to grind up tough leaves and branches. Bactrosaurus was about thirteen feet long. **Mid-Cretaceous**

Barapasaurus   (buh-RAP-uh-SORE-us)

One of the oldest known sauropods, Barapasaurus ("big-leg lizard") had a very long neck and probably stretched sixty feet from nose to tail. With its spoon-shaped teeth, this early dinosaur ate leaves and branches from the tops of trees. **Early Jurassic**

beak

A beak is a curved, pointed, horny structure on the mouth of an animal. It can be used to crush or cut food. Most birds have beaks. So did some dinosaurs.

Beak

biped   (BY-ped)

An animal that walks on two feet is a biped. Most meat-eating dinosaurs were bipeds.

Brachiosaurus   (BRAK-ee-o-SORE-us)

Brachiosaurus ("arm lizard") was a huge dinosaur that weighed eighty-five tons and was seventy-five feet long. Because of its very long neck and long front legs, Brachiosaurus was probably able to eat leaves from the tops of tall trees. This creature's nostrils were high on top of its head.
Late Jurassic

Brachyceratops   (brack-ee-SAIR-uh-tops)

Brachyceratops ("short-horned face") was a horned dinosaur. Although very small, the horns on its face may have been used as weapons. A short frill extended from the back of its head. For a Ceratopsian, this animal was small.
Like its relatives though, it ate plants.
Late Cretaceous

Brontosaurus   (BRON-toe-SORE-us)

See Apatosaurus.

browsers   (BROW-zerz)

Animals that eat the twigs and leaves of trees, shrubs, and other plants are browsers. Many dinosaurs were browsers.

Camarasaurus   (kam-AR-o-SORE-us)

Camarasaurus ("chambered lizard") was heavily built and between thirty and sixty feet long. It had blunt, forward-pointing teeth and probably ate leaves from trees or low bushes. The nostrils of the Camarasaurus were on top of its head. Some scientists think it may have even had a trunk.
Jurassic

Camptosaurus   (KAMP-toe-SORE-us)

This dinosaur had long legs, very short arms, and small hooves on its fingers and toes. It probably walked on two legs, but may have grazed on all four. The Camptosaurus ("bent reptile") was a twenty- three -foot-long plant-eater.
Late Jurassic/Early Cretaceous

Carcharodontosaurus
(kar-kar-o-DON-toe-SORE-us)

A large predator, the twenty-six-foot-long Carcharodontosaurus ("sharp-toothed lizard") had sharp, straight teeth and strong claws. It lived in what is now a part of the Sahara.
Early Cretaceous

carnivorous   (kar-NIV-or-us)

Any animal that eats mainly meat is carnivorous. Many dinosaurs ate other dinosaurs or other animals. They are called carnivorous dinosaurs.

carnosaurs   (KAR-no-sorz)

The word means flesh-eating. Dinosaurs that ate other animals are called carnosaurs. Carnosaurs walked on two legs and had sharp teeth and short arms with claws for gripping their prey.

Cenozoic era   (see-nuh-ZO-ik)

The Cenozoic era ("recent life") is a period of time that began 66 million years ago and continues to the present. Dinosaurs became extinct before the Cenozoic era began.

Centrosaurus   (sen-tro-SORE-us)

This dinosaur had an eighteen-inch, forward-curving horn on its snout. Its frill was lined with many knobs and tipped with two horns that also curved forward. The Centrosaurus ("sharp-point lizard") looked almost like a rhinoceros. It was twenty feet long, ate plants, and walked on all fours. **Cretaceous**

Ceratosaurus   (sair-AT-o-SORE-us)

A meat-eater, Ceratosaurus ("horned lizard") had a small horn on its nose, walked on its long hind legs, and was fifteen to twenty feet long from nose to tail. Its arms were short but powerful, and its fingers were tipped with sharp claws. This hunter was also equipped with many large, sharp teeth. **Late Jurassic**

Cetiosaurus   (SEAT-ee-o-SORE-us)

Cetiosaurus ("whale lizard") was a very big plant-eater. It was forty-five to sixty feet long and weighed more than ten tons. It had a long neck and tail, and its short, flat teeth were good for grinding up plants. **Late Jurassic**

Chasmosaurus   (KAZ-mo-SORE-us)

At seventeen feet long, Chasmosaurus ("cleft lizard") was a medium-sized dinosaur. It had a beak like a parrot's, which it used to snip leaves from plants. It had a long frill which protected its neck. Chasmosaurus had a small horn on its nose and two long horns above its eyes. It may have used these horns to defend itself. **Late Cretaceous**

claw

The pointed tip on an animal's fingers and toes is called a claw. Some dinosaurs had claws that were very long and sharp. Claws were used to grasp food and as a weapon for attack or defense.

Claw

Coelophysis   (seel-o-FY-sis)

About 220 million years ago, this slender creature was one of the first known dinosaurs to develop. It was about ten feet in length from its snout to the end of its long, thin tail. It had three strong fingers on each hand to grip the tiny lizards that it ate. Coelophysis ("hollow form") weighed less than 100 pounds. **Late Triassic**

10

coelurosaurs   (see-LURE-o-sorz)

Coelurosaurs ("hollow lizards") were fast, meat-eating dinosaurs. Their hollow, birdlike bones made these dinosaurs light and able to run quickly.

cold-blooded

When an animal's body temperature changes with the temperature of its environment, the animal is called cold-blooded. Birds and mammals, which have a constant body temperature, are called warm-blooded. Modern cold-blooded animals include fish, reptiles, and amphibians. Scientists are divided as to whether some dinosaurs were warm-blooded or cold-blooded.

11

Compsognathus   (komp-so-NAY-thus)

One of the smallest dinosaurs, two-and-a-half-foot-long
Compsognathus ("pretty jaw") had slender, birdlike legs.
Some scientists think it may have had feathers. When it ran,
this dinosaur held its long tail straight out for balance.
Compsognathus ate small lizards and insects. **Late Jurassic**

Corythosaurus   (ko-RITH-o-SORE-us)

This heavyset dinosaur had a large
crest on top of its head. The crest
looked like half a dinner plate set on
edge. Corythosaurus ("helmet lizard")
was a duck-billed plant-eater. It was
thirty-three feet long and weighed
more than four tons. **Late Cretaceous**

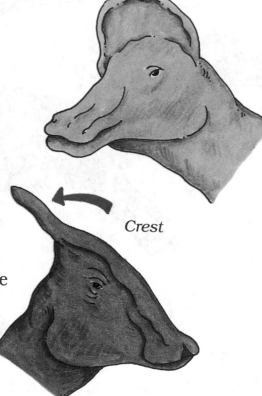

Crest

crest

A crest is a bony, skin-covered structure
on top of an animal's head. Many of the
duck-billed dinosaurs had crests. The size
and shape of the crest may have helped
these animals to recognize each other.

Cretaceous period   (kreh-TAY-shus)

The Cretaceous period was the final period in the Mesozoic era.
It began 142 million years ago and lasted for about 76 million
years. The first snakes and flowers appeared during this time.
The dinosaurs became extinct at the end of Cretaceous period
66 million years ago.

Daspletosaurus
(das-PLEET-o-SORE-us)

The twenty-eight-foot-long Daspleto-saurus ("frightful lizard") was a meat-eater and closely related to Tyranno-saurus. It had a giant head and long jaws with many sharp teeth. Its big tail helped to balance its large head. This animal's legs were strong and powerful, but its arms were short and thin. **Late Cretaceous**

Deinocheirus   (dine-o-KY-rus)

Deinocheirus ("terrible hand") had curved, ten-inch-long, razor-sharp claws for gripping and tearing prey. Although it is not certain how large this dinosaur was, its arms alone were more than eight feet long. **Late Cretaceous**

Deinonychus (di-NON-i-kus)

Deinonychus ("terrible claw") was a meat-eater with large teeth and powerful claws. Its name comes from the very large claw on the second toe of each hind foot. Deinonychus was able to pull these large claws up as it ran to keep them sharp. On the attack, the large claws could be snapped forward like switchblades. This fierce dinosaur was between ten and thirteen feet long. **Early Cretaceous**

Dimorphodon   (die-MOR-fo-don)

The Dimorphodon ("two-form tooth") was not a dinosaur but an early pterosaur. It had a big skull and sharp teeth. Its leathery wings were probably best suited for gliding rather than flying. Dimorphodon ate fish or lizards. **Jurassic**

dinosaur (DINE-o-sore)

The dinosaur ("terrible lizard") lived during the Mesozoic era. It was a land-dwelling branch of the archosaur family of reptiles. Unlike most reptiles of the period, dinosaurs had straight legs and walked with their bodies held up off the ground. They laid eggs, and some cared for their young.

Diplodocus   (di-PLOD-o-kus)

Diplodocus ("double beam") was a giant in the dinosaur world. It was eighty-eight feet long and yet, weighing about twelve tons, it was fairly light for its size. Its name refers to double skids on its tailbones, which could protect the very long tail if it was dragged on the ground. Diplodocus had a long, slender neck that enabled this plant-eater to reach leaves and branches at the tops of trees. **Late Jurassic**

Dromaeosaurus   (DROM-ee-o-SORE-us)

Dromaeosaurus ("running lizard") was a small dinosaur, measuring only six feet long, but it could run very fast. It was a meat-eater with large teeth and claws, including a three-inch claw on each hind foot. **Late Cretaceous**

Dromiceiomimus   (dro-MISS-ee-o-MIME-us)

The long, strong legs of Dromiceiomimus ("emu mimic") enabled it to run very fast. It may have been one of the fastest dinosaurs. It also had large eyes and a big brain for a dinosaur. It probably ate small animals, eggs, and fruit. Dromiceiomimus was about eleven feet long and resembled a modern ostrichlike bird called an emu. **Late Cretaceous**

Dryosaurus (dry-o-SORE-us)

This dinosaur had a birdlike beak to clip off the leaves of plants that it ate. Since it had no front teeth, it ground up its food with its back teeth. The Dryosaurus ("oak lizard") was about twelve feet long, four feet tall, and weighed about 170 pounds. **Late Jurassic/Early Cretaceous**

Dryptosaurus (drip-toe-SORE-us)

Dryptosaurus ("wounding lizard") had eight-inch-long claws. Its teeth were sharp. Although its exact size is not known, this dinosaur was probably more than twenty feet long. **Late Cretaceous**

Edmontosaurus
(ed-MON-toe-SORE-us)

Edmontosaurus ("Edmonton lizard") was a duck-billed dinosaur. It had about a thousand small teeth to grind up the plants it ate. This big dinosaur was about forty feet long and walked on two legs. **Late Cretaceous**

Efraasia (eh-FRAH-see-a)

Efraasia ("of E. Fraas") was named for the man who discovered it. It was an early, eight-foot-long plant-eater that walked often on two legs and sometimes on all four. **Late Triassic**

Euoplocephalus
(you-op-luh-SEF-uh-lus)

Euoplocephalus ("well-armored head") was one of the largest ankylosaurs. It weighed about two tons and was about twenty feet long. It was built like a tank, with bony bands of armor and rows of five-inch-long spikes down its back. It also had a club with two spikes at the end of its tail to hit attackers. **Late Cretaceous**

evolution (ev-o-LOO-shun)

Most scientists believe that animals change in form over millions of years. This process of slow change is called evolution.

extinct (ek-STINKT)

When an entire group of animals dies out completely it becomes extinct. It is gone forever. The dinosaurs became extinct 66 million years ago. No one is sure why this happened.

Fabrosaurus   (fab-ro-SORE-us)

Fabrosaurus ("Fabre's lizard") was a small three-foot-long dinosaur. It had strong teeth with knobby edges and was probably a plant-eater.
Triassic

family

A group of animals that have many features in common is a family. Dinosaurs with duck bills, for example, were members of the hadrosaurid family.

fang

Fangs are long, pointed teeth that are used for stabbing or tearing.

Fang

foliage   (FO-lee-ij)

The leaves and branches of plants are foliage. This was an important source of food for many dinosaurs.

fossil

Any trace of a living thing that has been preserved is a fossil. Fossils can be the actual remains of an animal or plant, imprints of its parts, or even footprints.

frill

The ceratopsid family of dinosaurs, which included Triceratops, had a bony structure called a frill on the back of their skulls. This frill protected the neck and part of the back. Sometimes the frill had holes in it, which made it lighter. The surface was probably covered with skin.

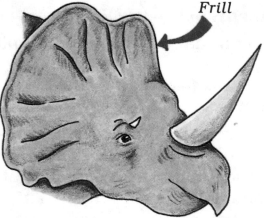

Frill

gastrolith (GAS-tro-lith)

Some dinosaurs did not chew their food. Instead, they swallowed small rocks, which would grind up the food once it was in their stomach. These rocks are sometimes found with dinosaur fossils and are called gastroliths ("stomach stones").

geologist (gee-OL-o-gist)

A person who studies the earth is a geologist. Layers of the earth in which fossils are discovered can give clues as to when the animals lived and what the environment was like at that time.

Hadrosaurus (had-row-SORE-us)

Hadrosaurus ("bulky lizard") was about thirty feet long. It was a duck-billed dinosaur with a wide, flat mouth. This creature probably relied on keen senses of sight, hearing, and smell to avoid predators. **Late Cretaceous**

herbivore   (HERB-ih-vor)

An animal that eats mainly plants is called a herbivore.

Heterodontosaurus
(het-er-o-DON-toe-SORE-us)

Heterodontosaurus ("different-toothed lizard") had different types of teeth, some for cutting leaves and plants, and some for grinding them. This four-foot-long dinosaur probably used its tiny hands to pull branches within reach of its mouth. **Late Triassic**

Homalocephale   (hoe-mal-o-SEF-a-lee)

This dinosaur had a flat head with many knobs and bumps on each side. A plant-eater, Homalocephale ("even head") was about ten feet long. **Late Cretaceous**

hoof

The hoof is a flat, horny structure on the fingers and toes of an animal. It protects the hands and feet. Modern cows and horses have hooves, and so did many dinosaurs.

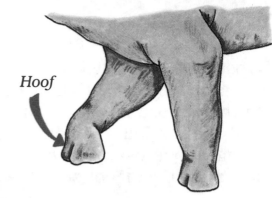

Hoof

Hoplitosaurus   (hop-LEE-toe-SORE-us)

Hoplitosaurus ("armed lizard") was named after the ancient Greek foot soldier, hoplite, because, like a soldier, it had excellent armor. The dinosaur's armor covered its head, back, and tail. Hoplitosaurus had small, weak teeth and probably ate soft plants. **Early Cretaceous**

horn

A hard, usually pointed structure that grows from an animal's head is called a horn. Horns have a bony core, with a tough covering of hard skin or hair. Many dinosaurs had horns, and they may have used them as weapons.

Hylaeosaurus   (HI-lee-o-SORE-us)

Hylaeosaurus ("woodland lizard"), also known as Polacanthus, walked on all four feet. An armored dinosaur, it was well protected by spikes that lined its sides and covered its back and tail. Like other ankylosaurs, fifteen-foot-long Hylaeosaurus ate plants. **Early Cretaceous**

Hypacrosaurus
(hi-PAK-row-SORE-us)

Hypacrosaurus ("high-ranked lizard") was a member of the duck-bill family. On this dinosaur's head was a small crest that ended in a bony spike. Plant-eating Hypacrosaurus was thirty feet long. **Late Cretaceous**

Hypsilophodon (hip-sih-LOAF-o-don)

This small dinosaur was between five and seven feet long. It ate plants that it clipped with its bony beak. A fast runner, Hypsilophodon ("high-ridged tooth") held its long tail high and straight for balance. **Early Cretaceous**

Ichthyosaurus (ick-thee-o-SORE-us)

This seagoing reptile lived during the age of the dinosaurs. Ichthyosaurus ("fish lizard") looked like a dolphin and most likely ate fish. Some may have been thirty feet long, but most were much smaller. **Mesozoic**

Iguanodon   (ee-GWAN-o-don)

The first scientists to examine the fossils of twenty-five- to thirty-foot-long Iguanodon ("iguana tooth") thought it had a horn on its nose. Later they discovered that this plant-eater actually had *two* sharp, bony spikes that belonged on its thumbs.
Early Cretaceous

insectivore   (in-SEK-tih-vor)

Animals that eat mainly insects are called insectivores. Many small, fast dinosaurs were insectivores.

Jurassic period   (jur-ASS-ick)

The Jurassic period was the middle period of the Mesozoic era. It began about 208 million years ago and lasted for about 66 million years. Some of the largest dinosaurs lived during this time.

Kentrosaurus (ken-tro-SORE-us)

Kentrosaurus ("pointed lizard") was an armor-plated dinosaur. It had many pairs of short, triangle-shaped plates on its back. Sharp spines ran from the middle of its back to the tip of its tail. At sixteen feet long, Kentrosaurus was one of the smallest members of its family of stegosaurids. **Late Jurassic**

Lambeosaurus (lam-bee-o-SORE-us)

This member of the duck-bill family had a crest that was shaped like a hatchet with a bony spike at the back. Lambeosaurus ("Lambe's lizard") was about forty-five feet long. It ate pine needles, twigs, and leaves. **Late Cretaceous**

Lesothosaurus
(leh-SOTH-o-SORE-us)

This small dinosaur was only three feet long. Lesothosaurus ("Lesotho lizard") had long, slender legs and could run very fast. A plant-eater, it probably relied on speed to avoid predators. **Late Triassic/Early Jurassic**

Mamenchisaurus   (ma-MEN-chee-SORE-us)

This dinosaur had the longest neck of any animal that ever lived, more than thirty-three feet. From nose to tail, plant-eating Mamenchisaurus ("Mamenchi lizard") was more than seventy-five feet long. **Late Jurassic**

Megalosaurus   (MEG-uh-low-SORE-us)

Megalosaurus ("great lizard") was a thirty-foot-long predator. It had long, powerful legs, short arms, and sharp claws. This fierce dinosaur's teeth were jagged-edged for slicing through flesh. Megalosaurus was the first dinosaur to be named. **Early Jurassic/Early Cretaceous**

25

Mesozoic era   (mez-o-ZO-ik)

The Mesozoic era ("age of middle life") is a period of Earth's history that began 245 million years ago and ended 66 million years ago. The dinosaurs lived during the Mesozoic era.

mosasaurs   (MOZE-uh-sorz)

Mosasaurs ("Meuse lizards") were not dinosaurs, but thirty-foot-long, seagoing lizards. Like most predators, they had long, sharp teeth. Mosasaurs used their tail and paddlelike feet for swimming. They probably ate fish and other reptiles. **Late Cretaceous**

Mussaurus   (moose-SORE-us)

Mussaurus ("mouse lizard") is the smallest dinosaur yet discovered. The fossil remains found were of a nestling only eight inches long, about the size of a kitten. Adult Mussaurus may have been much larger. **Late Triassic**

Muttaburrasaurus (MUT-uh-BUR-uh-SORE-us)

Muttaburrasaurus ("Muttaburra lizard") was named after the place in Australia where its remains were found. Its teeth show that it might have had a varied diet, but probably usually ate plants. This dinosaur was twenty-three feet long and had spiked thumbs. **Cretaceous**

Noasaurus (no-uh-SORE-us)

Though only six feet long, Noasaurus ("northwestern Argentina lizard") was a fierce hunter. It had a long, curved claw on its middle toe that could be used like a knife to slash and tear at its prey. **Late Cretaceous**

Nodosaurus (no-doe-SORE-us)

The back and tail of Nodosaurus ("node lizard") were covered with bony knobs and plates. It may have also had small, protective spines. Like other ankylosaurs, eighteen-foot-long Nodosaurus had short legs and probably browsed on plants growing close to the ground. **Cretaceous**

omnivorous (om-NIV-or-us)

Some animals eat both plants and other animals. Omnivorous means "eats everything." Many dinosaurs were omnivorous.

Opisthocoelicaudia   (o-PIS-tho-SEAL-ih-KAW-dee-uh)

Opisthocoelicaudia ("backward hollow tail") walked on all fours with its tail held up off the ground. Using its long tail for balance, this large reptile may have stood on its hind legs to reach leaves in the treetops. **Late Cretaceous**

ornithischians   (ore-nih-THISS-kee-anz)

Most ornithischians ("bird hipped") were herbivores and had parrotlike beaks to snip and cut leaves and twigs of the plants they ate. They had flat teeth to grind the foliage. Ornithopods, stegosaurs, ankylosaurs, and ceratopsids were all ornithischians.

ornithopods   (ore-NITH-o-PODZ)

These dinosaurs were herbivores. Most were medium-sized and walked on their hind legs. Ornithopods ("bird feet") probably had keen senses. Their best defense against predators was to avoid them. Iguanodon, Anatosaurus, and Lambeosaurus were included in this group.

Ouranosaurus   (or-RAN-o-SORE-us)

The Ouranosaurus (''brave lizard'') was about twenty-three feet long. It may have had a ''sail'' of skin on its back that could be used as a heat exchanger to maintain its body temperature. The Ouranosaurus was a plant-eating dinosaur. **Early Cretaceous**

Oviraptor   (O-vi-RAP-tor)

The Oviraptor (''egg thief'') was an unusual dinosaur. It did not have teeth, and may have eaten other dinosaurs' eggs, which it would crush with its jaw. Oviraptor was about six feet long. **Late Cretaceous**

Pachycephalosaurus
(pak-ee-SEF-uh-low-SORE-us)

The top of Pachycephalosaurus' (''thick-headed reptile'') skull was more than nine inches thick. The teeth show that it was a plant-eater. It is possible that these fifteen-foot-long dinosaurs butted heads with each other to establish dominance within the herd. **Late Cretaceous**

paleontologist   (pay-lee-on-TOL-ah-jist)

A paleontologist is a scientist who studies fossils to learn about ancient life.

Pangaea   (pan-JEE-uh)

The scientists who study changes in the earth's crust think that all the continents were once linked together in one big "supercontinent." Pangaea ("all-earth") broke up into separate continents and began to drift apart during the Triassic period.

Panoplosaurus   (pan-OP-la-SORE-us)

The Panoplosaurus ("fully armored lizard") had hard armor plates all over its body. This twenty-three-foot-long dinosaur had short legs and probably fed on low-lying plants.
Late Cretaceous

Parasaurolophus
(par-uh-SORE-o-LOAF-us)

This member of the duck-bill family had the most unusual crest of any dinosaur. It was a long hollow tube that stuck out five feet from the back of its head. The Parasaurolophus ("similar-crested lizard") was a thirty-three-foot-long plant-eater.
Late Cretaceous

30

Pentaceratops (pen-tuh-SAIR-uh-tops)

Pentaceratops means "five-horned face." Two horns grew from the top of its head, a smaller one on its nose, and a hornlike growth on each cheek. It also had a frill with small bones all around the edge. This plant-eating dinosaur was twenty-three feet long. **Late Cretaceous**

phytosaurs (FIE-toe-sorz)

Phytosaur means "plant lizard," but these creatures did not eat plants. Not true dinosaurs, these reptiles, which looked similar to crocodiles, had sharp teeth and were meat-eaters. Phytosaurs grew to be from ten to thirty feet long and lived in marshes, lakes, and streams. **Late Triassic**

Pinacosaurus (Pin-AK-o-SORE-us)

Pinacosaurus ("plank lizard") was a medium-sized dinosaur, about eighteen feet long. It had weak teeth, so it may have eaten soft plants. The tail ended in a large, bony club. Perhaps Pinacosaurus defended itself by swinging its tail at an attacker. **Late Cretaceous**

plate

A plate is a body structure embedded in or protruding from the skin. No one knows for sure how plates were attached to the dinosaurs that had them or in which direction they pointed. Some scientists think that plates may have been heat exchangers to maintain body temperature.

Plateosaurus
(PLAY-tee-o-SORE-us)

This large twenty-nine-foot dinosaur browsed on the leaves of tall trees. Its long neck would help it reach high branches, and it probably stood on its hind legs to make eating from trees easier. The Plateosaurus ("flat lizard") had a large, curved claw on its thumb that may have been used to defend it against predators. **Late Triassic**

Plesiosaurus (PLEE-zee-o-SORE-us)

Plesiosaurus ("near lizard") was a marine reptile which swam through the water with large, well-developed flippers. Fish-eating Plesiosaurus had a long neck and short tail, and was about ten feet long, but some may have been even bigger. **Jurassic**

Polacanthus (po-la-KAN-thus)

See Hylaeosaurus.

predator (PRED-uh-tor)

Any animal that hunts and kills other animals is a predator. Many dinosaurs, such as Allosaurus and Deinonychus, were predators.

prey

The animal that a predator hunts is called its prey. To hunt, catch, and eat an animal is to prey upon it.

Proganochelys (pro-gan-o-SHE-liss)

The Proganochelys (''first turtle'') was a reptile that lived about 210 million years ago, near the beginning of the age of dinosaurs. It had a thick shell to protect its body, but unlike most modern turtles it probably could not draw its head into its shell. **Triassic**

Protoceratops (pro-toe-SAIR-uh-tops)

Protoceratops ("first horned face") was a horned dinosaur. It was a small plant-eater, about six feet long. Both males and females had a bony frill that protected their necks. But only the males had a raised bump on their snouts. Many fossils and eggs of the Protoceratops have been found. **Late Cretaceous**

Protosuchus   (pro-toe-SOOK-us)

Protosuchus ("first crocodile") lived at the same time as the dinosaur and was the ancestor of modern crocodiles. It was small, about three feet long, and walked like a dog. Protosuchus ate small animals and may have spent much of its time on land. **Late Triassic**

Psittacosaurus (sih-TAK-o-SORE-us)

Scientists think the Psittacosaurus ("parrot lizard") walked on its hind legs. About six feet long, this animal had a parrotlike beak for clipping the leaves from plants. Psittacosaurus had a very slight frill. **Early Cretaceous**

Pterodactyl   (tair-o-DAK-til)

The pterodactyl ("wing finger") was not a dinosaur. It had leathery wings and could fly. Because it had very weak back legs, it may have been clumsy on land. The pterodactyl ate insects and fish. **Late Jurassic**

pterosaurs   (TAIR-o-sorz)

Pterosaurs ("wing lizards") were a group of flying reptiles that lived at the time of the dinosaurs. The pterodactyl was one kind of pterosaur. There were many others. Early pterosaurs were very small, but later ones were larger, with wing spans of up to forty feet. **Late Triassic/Late Cretaceous**

quadruped   (KWAD-roo-ped)

A quadruped is an animal that walks on all four legs. Modern dogs and cats are quadrupeds. People are bipeds. Many dinosaurs, especially the largest ones, were quadrupeds.

reptile   (REP-tile)

Reptiles are cold-blooded animals that breathe air. They have scaly, water-resistant skin. Most reptiles lay eggs protected by a shell. Dinosaurs were a kind of reptile.

rhynchosaurs   (RIN-ko-sorz)

Rhynchosaurs had beaklike upper jaws. These small dinosaurs were about six feet long but had mouths very large for their size. Most rhynchosaurs are extinct, but there is still one kind that is alive today. It is a strange little lizard called a tuatara. **Late Triassic**

Saltasaurus   (salt-uh-SORE-us)

Thousands of small bones on the skin of the Saltasaurus ("Salta lizard") formed an armored plate to protect it. It was forty feet long and ate plants. Although it usually walked on all four of its elephantlike legs, it may have been able to rear up on its hind legs to reach leaves high in the treetops. **Late Cretaceous**

saurischian (sore-ISS-kee-an)

This is a large group of dinosaurs. The saurischian ("lizard hip") dinosaurs had lizardlike hips and claws on their feet. Many walked on their hind legs, but some walked on all fours. Many of the saurischians were fierce meat-eaters, others ate plants, and some ate both. The very large sauropods were in this group.

Saurolophus (sore-o-LOAF-us)

This member of the duck-bill family had a ridge along the top of its head with a bony spike protruding from the back. Saurolophus ("crested lizard") was more than thirty feet long. **Late Cretaceous**

sauropods (SORE-o-podz)

Sauropods ("lizard feet") were the giants in the dinosaur family. Some were as big as 100 feet long and weighed up to 150 tons. Sauropods were herbivores and walked on all four legs. Diplodocus, Apatosaurus, and Brachiosaurus were sauropods.

Saurornithoides (sore-or-nith-OY-deez)

This quick-moving meat-eater was six feet long and had large eyes and a big brain for a dinosaur. It could probably see well at night and judge distances well. Saurornithoides ("birdlike lizard") probably used its long arms and grasping hands to catch and hold small mammals that came out to feed at dusk. **Late Cretaceous**

scavenger (SKAV-en-jer)

Many large, meat-eating dinosaurs did not kill the animals they ate. They ate animals that were already dead. An animal that eats whatever it finds is called a scavenger. Some scientists think the Tyrannosaurus may have been a scavenger.

Scelidosaurus (skel-IDE-o-SORE-us)

Fossils of the plant-eater Scelidosaurus ("limb lizard") indicate that this dinosaur had many small, bony knobs and spikes on the skin that acted as armor. The Scelidosaurus was a thirteen-foot-long quadruped. **Early Jurassic**

37

Scutellosaurus
(skoo-TEL-o-SORE-us)

The skin of Scutellosaurus ("small shield lizard") was covered with hundreds of protective bony knobs. This four-foot-long dinosaur had a very long tail, twice as long as its body and neck together. It was a plant-eater and could probably run fast on its hind legs or walk on all four legs. **Early Jurassic**

Segnosaurus (seg-no-SORE-us)

Segnosaurus ("slow lizard") was a thirty-foot-long carnivore but was built more like a plant-eating dinosaur. It probably ate fish. It had a beak instead of front teeth and had three-fingered hands and four toes on each foot with long, curved claws. **Late Cretaceous**

skull

The bones of an animal's head make up the skull. By studying the skull, scientists learn what animals probably ate. They can also discover how smart an animal may have been by the size of the opening inside the skull, which held the brain. Compared to modern mammals, even large dinosaurs had very small brains.

Spinosaurus (spy-no-SORE-us)

This meat-eating dinosaur had a row of six-foot-tall spines on its back that were probably covered by skin to form a sail. Some scientists think that forty-foot-long Spinosaurus ("spiny lizard") used the sail to regulate body temperature. It may have turned the sail toward the sun to warm up and away from the sun to cool down.
Late Cretaceous

Staurikosaurus (store-ick-o-SORE-us)

This dinosaur was six feet long but weighed only about sixty-five pounds. Staurikosaurus ("cross lizard") was a fast-moving hunter with long, slender legs and many curved teeth to hold and tear at its prey. **Mid to Late Triassic**

Stegoceras (steg-OSS-air-us)

The Stegoceras ("covered horn") had a very thick dome on the top of its skull. It was a small dinosaur, only six feet long. It walked on its hind legs and was a plant-eater. **Late Cretaceous**

Stegosaurus (steg-o-SORE-us)

The Stegosaurus ("plated lizard") was up to thirty feet long and weighed up to two tons. It had large, triangle-shaped plates on its back. These plates may have helped regulate its body temperature. On its tail were four sharp spikes for defense. Stegosaurus was an herbivore. **Late Jurassic**

Stenonychosaurus   (sten-ON-ik-o-SORE-us)

Stenonychosaurus ("narrow claw lizard") had large eyes and a big brain for a dinosaur. Some scientists think it may have been the most intelligent dinosaur. This six-foot-long, lightly built reptile could run fast on its strong legs. A meat-eater, it had long, sharp claws to grasp its prey. **Late Cretaceous**

Struthiomimus
(STREW-thee-o-MY-mus)

Struthiomimus ("ostrich mimic") was about twelve feet long and looked something like a very large, featherless ostrich. It had strong arms and hands with powerful curved claws. This dinosaur was probably fast and preyed upon small animals. It may have also eaten plants and fruit. **Late Cretaceous**

Struthiosaurus (STREW-thee-o-SORE-us)

Struthiosaurus ("ostrich lizard") had armor down its back from its neck to its tail. At only six feet long, it was small compared to other armored dinosaurs. This little reptile was a plant-eater. **Late Cretaceous**

Styracosaurus (sty-RAK-o-SORE-us)

Six long spikes lined the edge of the frill on this dinosaur. Styracosaurus ("spiked lizard") also had a long horn on its snout. It was a medium-sized dinosaur measuring about eighteen feet long. Styracosaurus was a plant-eater. **Late Cretaceous**

Supersaurus (soo-per-SORE-us)

This giant was almost 100 feet long and may have weighed more than seventy-five tons. Supersaurus ("super lizard") had a very long neck, and could raise its head nearly five stories high, about fifty feet. It could easily browse for leaves at the treetops. **Late Jurassic**

talon

The claw of a predator is called a talon. Many dinosaurs had long, sharp talons.

Tanystropheus (tan-ee-STRO-fee-us)

Tanystropheus ("long vertebrae") was not a dinosaur but a strange-looking lizard that lived 200 million years ago. It was twenty-one feet long, but most of that was neck and tail. It lived near water and probably ate fish. **Triassic**

Tarchia   (TAR-kee-uh)

Tarchia ("brainy") was a large armored ankylosaur. It was twenty-eight feet long. Armor plates and rows of spikes ran down its back to its clubbed tail. The Tarchia had weak teeth and probably ate soft plants. **Late Cretaceous**

Tenontosaurus
(ten-ON-toe-SORE-us)

Tenontosaurus ("sinew lizard") was a sturdily built, medium-sized herbivore. It was more than twenty feet long. This animal's very long tail may have been used for defense.
Early Cretaceous

42

Teratosaurus   (teh-RAT-o-SORE-us)

Even though Teratosaurus ("monster lizard") was twenty feet long, it weighed less than a ton. It had strong arms and legs and could run quickly. This dinosaur was equipped with sharp teeth and claws for tearing its food apart. **Late Triassic**

Thecodontosaurus   (thee-ko-DON-toe-SORE-us)

This small, seven-foot-long dinosaur was omnivorous. Thecodontosaurus ("socket-tooth lizard") had many leaflike teeth for chewing both plants and meat. It had large claws that might have been used for digging or tearing at food. **Late Triassic/Early Jurassic**

thecodonts   (THEE-ko-dontz)

Thecodonts ("socket tooth") were reptiles that lived before the dinosaurs and are probably their ancestors. It is likely that the thecodonts were also the ancestors of crocodiles and birds. **Triassic**

theropod   (THER-o-pod)

Theropod ("beast foot") is the name of a large group of dinosaurs that had feet with three forward-pointing toes and one toe that pointed backward. These dinosaurs also had clawed hands. Most were bipedal and carnivorous. Allosaurus, Tyrannosaurus, and Compsognathus were members of this group.

Thescelosaurus   (THES-el-o-SORE-us)

The long, stiff tail of Thescelosaurus ("wonderful lizard") helped to keep its balance when it ran on its strong hind legs. The five-fingered hand may have been used to grasp branches. Thescelosaurus was about eleven feet long and it probably ate plants.
Late Cretaceous

Titanosaurus   (tie-TAN-o-SORE-us)

The Titanosaurus ("very large lizard") was a large-sized dinosaur, but scientists disagree about its size. It may have been from forty feet long to more than sixty feet long. This dinosaur had a very long tail that may have been used like a whip for protection.
Late Cretaceous

44

Torosaurus (tore-o-SORE-us)

The skull of the Torosaurus ("perforated lizard"), including its long frill, was as big as a car. The whole dinosaur was twenty to twenty-five feet long. It had two large horns above its eyes and a shorter horn on its nose. It used its parrotlike beak to clip the leaves of the plants it ate. **Late Cretaceous**

Triassic period (try-ASS-ick)

The Triassic period was the first and shortest period of the Mesozoic era. It began about 245 million years ago and lasted approximately 35 million years. The first dinosaurs developed during this time. The first shrewlike mammals also appeared at the end of this time.

Triceratops (try-SAIR-uh-tops)

Triceratops ("three-horned face") had three horns on its head. Over its eyes were two horns, each more than three feet long, and on its snout was a shorter horn. This thirty-foot-long dinosaur also had a frill on the back of its head, which protected its neck. Triceratops was a plant-eater and was among the very last dinosaurs to become extinct. **Late Cretaceous**

Troödon (TROE-o-don)

Troödon ("wounding tooth") was related to plant-eating dinosaurs, but it had the teeth of a meat-eater. The teeth were shaped like small "steak knives" with rough edges. Troödon was eight feet long. **Late Cretaceous**

Tsintaosaurus (chin-TAY-o-SORE-us)

Tsintaosaurus ("Tsintao lizard") was a member of the duck-bill family. A hollow, spikelike bone protruded from its head as a crest. This thirty-three-foot-long dinosaur was a plant-eater. **Late Cretaceous**

Tuojiangosaurus (too-HWANG-o-SORE-us)

A relative of Stegosaurus, this dinosaur had triangle-shaped plates on its back and spikes on its tail. A plant-eater, Tuojiangosaurus ("Tuo Jiang lizard") was twenty-three feet long. **Late Jurassic**

Tyrannosaurus
(tie-RAN-o-SORE-us)

Tyrannosaurus ("tyrant lizard") was a giant meat-eating dinosaur. It was forty-six feet long. This fierce animal's hind legs were powerful and long, but the arms were very small. Its strong jaws were lined with sharp, serrated teeth, some six inches long. Some scientists think Tyrannosaurus may have been a scavenger rather than a hunter. **Late Cretaceous**

Ultrasaurus   (ul-tra-SORE-us)

The Ultrasaurus ("ultra lizard") may have been the largest dinosaur of all. Fossils show it was more than ninety-eight feet long and may have weighed from 80 to 130 tons. This giant plant-eater probably had to browse continuously to survive. **Late Jurassic**

47

Velociraptor   (veh-LOSS-ih-RAP-tor)

The Velociraptor ("swift plunderer") was a small, fast predator. It had sharp claws on its hands for gripping prey and sharp teeth that were good for tearing at its food. Velociraptor was six feet long. **Late Cretaceous**

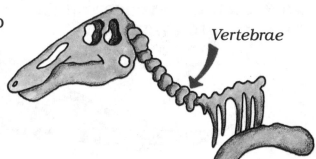

vertebrates   (VER-teh-braytz)

Animals with a backbone are called vertebrates. The backbone is made up of a row of hollow bones called vertebrae. The size of the vertebrae helps scientists decide how large an animal might have been. Dinosaurs were vertebrates.

Vertebrae